THE SELFIE MASTERPIECE

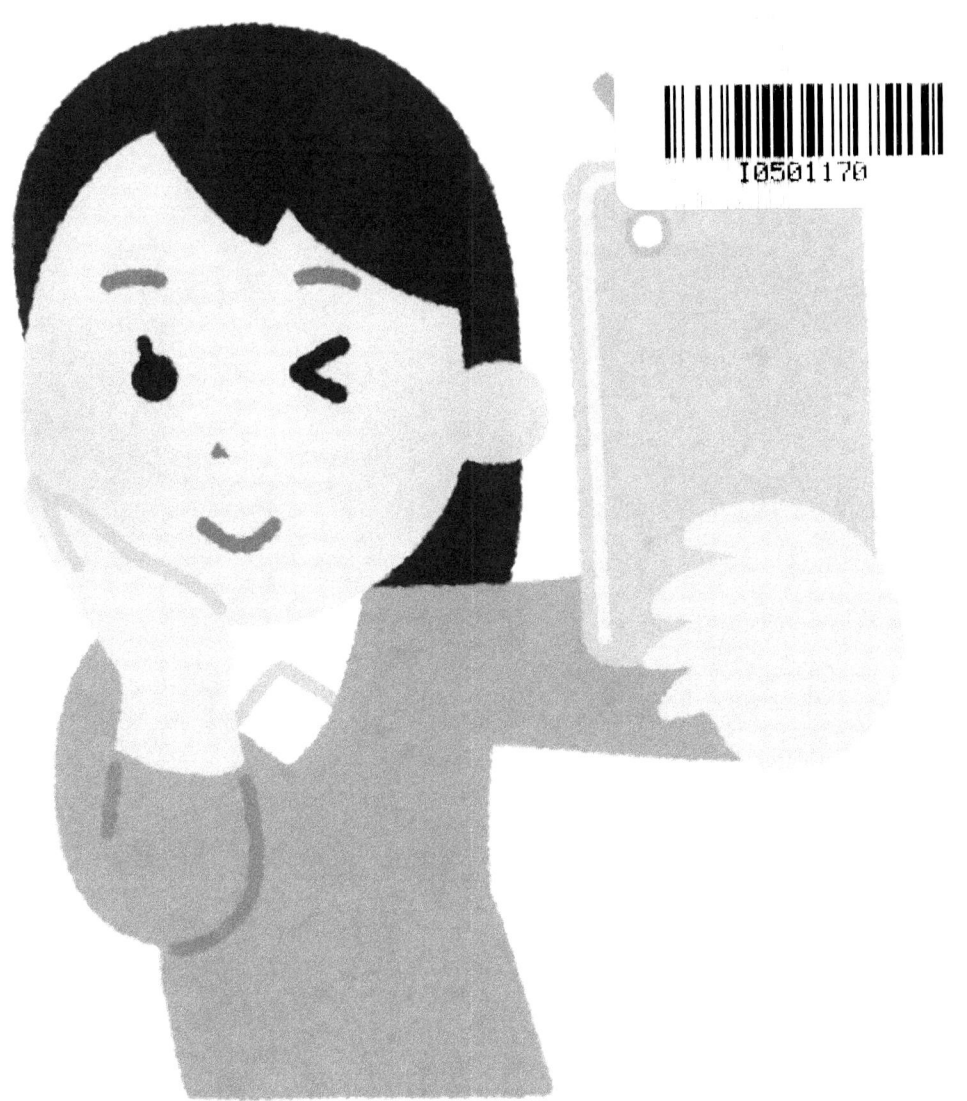

Secrets, Stories, and Skills to Capture Your Best Self

Copyright © 2024 O.Naumchyk
All rights reserved. No part of this book may be reproduced, distributed, or transmitted in any form or by any means, including photocopying, recording, or other electronic or mechanical methods, without the prior written permission of the author, except as allowed by copyright law.
Every image, design, and piece of content within this book is safeguarded by copyright and is the sole property of the author.

CONTENTS OF THE BOOK:

Introduction: The Power of a Selfie
1-4

Chapter 1: The Selfie Revolution
5-8

Chapter 2: 100 Secrets to Selfie Perfection
9-25

Chapter 3: Telling Your Story Through Selfies
26-31

Chapter 4: Programs and Apps for the Perfect Selfie
32-39

Chapter 5: 100 Surprising, Shocking, and Delightful Facts About Selfies
40-56

Final Part: The Art of Being Seen
57-59

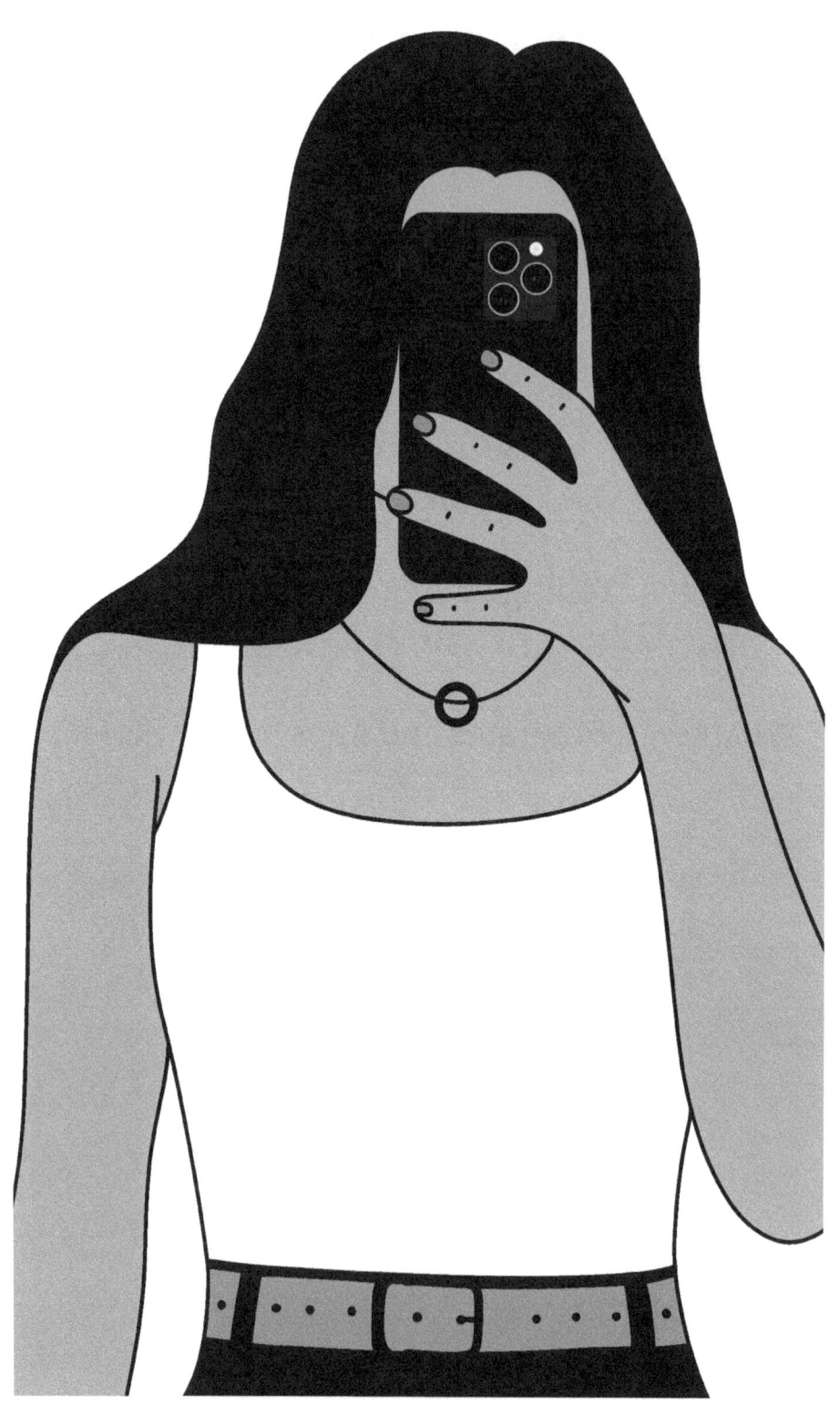

INTRODUCTION: THE POWER OF A SELFIE

Once upon a time, a photograph required a cumbersome camera, a patient photographer, and plenty of luck. Fast forward to today, and the act of taking a picture has transformed into an empowering ritual—a moment of self-expression, creativity, and connection. Welcome to the world of selfies, where everyone has the power to be their own artist, muse, and storyteller.

In this book, The Selfie Masterpiece: Secrets, Stories, and Skills to Capture Your Best Self, we're diving headfirst into the fascinating universe of selfies. Whether it's a casual snapshot, a playful filter experiment, or an awe-inspiring capture of you against the Grand Canyon's majestic cliffs, selfies have become an art form that's uniquely personal and undeniably universal.

But let's be honest: selfies are more than just pictures. They're a mirror of who we are and how we want to be seen by the world. They celebrate our individuality, our quirks, and the stories we want to tell. They're about capturing confidence, sharing joy, and sometimes even poking fun at ourselves.

This book isn't just about taking great selfies —it's about understanding their cultural impact, exploring the creativity behind every click, and embracing the journey of self-expression.

Here's what you can expect as you flip through these pages:
- Proven Tips and Techniques: From finding the perfect lighting to mastering your angles, you'll learn over 100 secrets to transform your selfies into scroll-stopping works of art.
- Intriguing Stories and Facts: Did you know that selfies date back to the 19th century? Or that astronauts, celebrities, and even gorillas have gone viral for their selfies? You'll uncover 100 fascinating, shocking, and hilarious selfie stories.
- Cutting-Edge Tools and Apps: Discover the technology behind the perfect selfie, from AI-enhanced editing tools to creative apps that bring your vision to life.
- Inspiration Galore: Whether you're capturing a special moment, experimenting with artistic styles, or telling a story through your selfies, this book will fuel your imagination.

So, whether you're here to boost your Instagram game, celebrate your unique style, or simply have fun, this book is your ultimate guide to the selfie revolution. Together, we'll explore how to take selfies that not only look amazing but also feel authentically you.

Let's get started on your journey to creating selfies that inspire, connect, and wow the world. The camera is ready, the lighting is perfect—now it's time to shine.

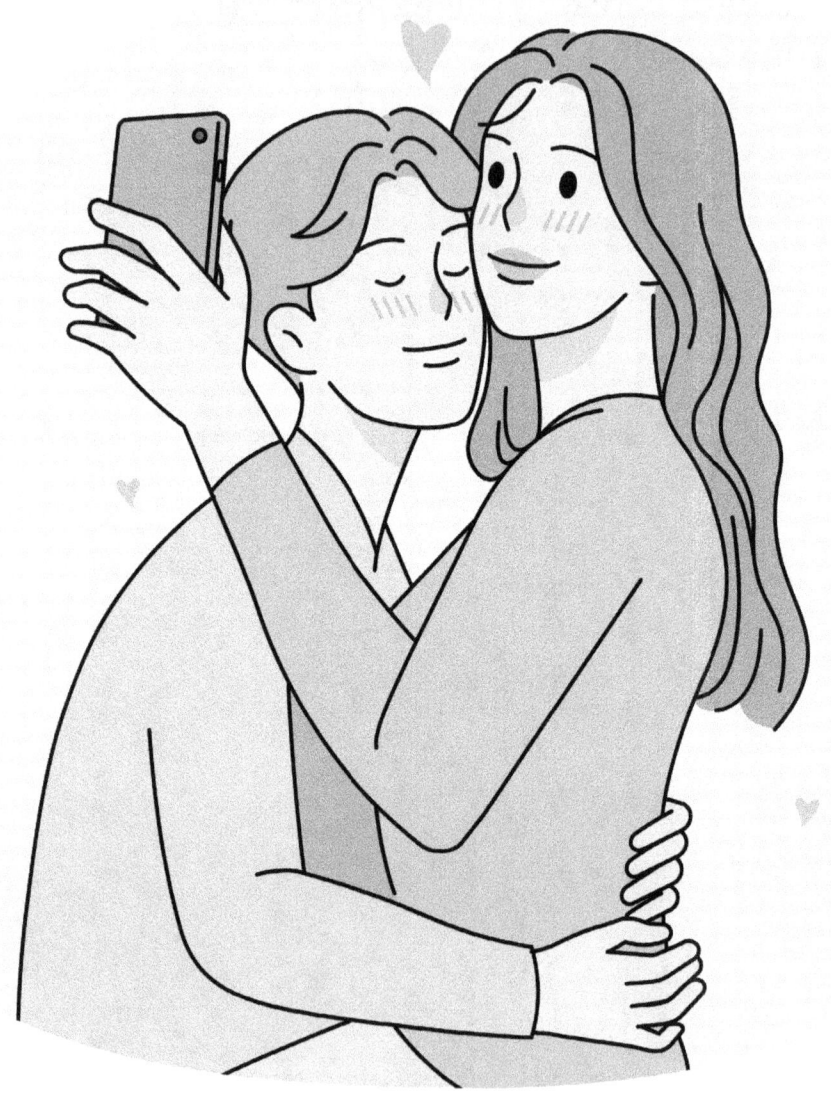

CHAPTER 1: THE SELFIE REVOLUTION

Not so long ago, capturing a photograph of oneself was a task reserved for clunky cameras and mirrored experiments.

Today, it has evolved into a cultural phenomenon that bridges self-expression, artistry, and technology. From casual snapshots to highly curated photo shoots, selfies have transformed how we see and present ourselves to the world.

In this chapter, we will explore the evolution of selfies, their significance in modern culture, and the foundational elements of a great selfie.

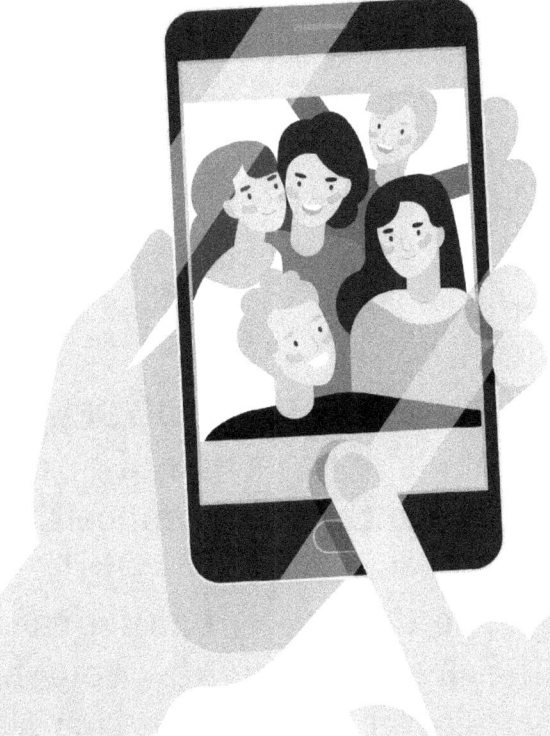

THE RISE OF THE SELFIE

The term "selfie" was first coined in 2002 on an Australian internet forum but didn't gain global prominence until over a decade later. The advent of smartphones equipped with front-facing cameras turned an ordinary habit into a global trend. Suddenly, anyone could be both the photographer and the subject. This shift wasn't just technological—it signaled a deeper cultural change, where individuality and personal storytelling became cornerstones of digital life.

But why has the selfie captivated us so deeply? Some say it's the perfect blend of control and creativity. With a selfie, you decide how to frame yourself, how to light the shot, and how to express your mood. It's both an art form and a personal statement. Whether you're at the Eiffel Tower, celebrating a birthday, or just feeling particularly good about your outfit, selfies let you immortalize the moment and share it instantly with the world.

THE SCIENCE OF A GOOD SELFIE

Every great selfie has a mix of three essential ingredients: lighting, composition, and authenticity. Let's unpack these a little.

Lighting: The quality of lighting can make or break a selfie. Ever noticed how your face looks radiant in natural sunlight? That's because natural light softens features, evens out skin tone, and adds a lively glow. On the flip side, harsh indoor lighting or shadows can dull your features. Learning how to find and use flattering light is the first step to mastering the selfie.

Composition: Selfies aren't just snapshots; they're mini works of art. How you frame yourself in the picture can make a dramatic difference. The rule of thirds—an age-old photography principle—can help balance your photo. By placing your face slightly off-center or aligning your eyes with the top third of the frame, you can create a visually appealing composition.

Authenticity: No filter can replace the power of a genuine smile or a natural pose. The best selfies often reflect a slice of real life—whether it's a candid laugh, a thoughtful gaze, or a silly moment with friends. Authenticity resonates more than perfection.

THE SOCIAL POWER OF SELFIES

Selfies are more than just photos; they're digital postcards that connect us to a wider community. Whether you're sharing a moment of pride, humor, or introspection, selfies offer a way to build connections and express individuality. They've also become powerful tools for self-confidence, as people celebrate their unique beauty and identities in a world that often pushes conformity.

However, selfies have their challenges too. The desire for the "perfect" shot can sometimes create pressure, leading to countless retakes or heavy editing. This chapter encourages you to embrace the imperfections, because the most memorable selfies are often the ones that tell a story—your story.

A WINDOW TO THE WORLD

From celebrities on red carpets to hikers at breathtaking summits, selfies have given us glimpses into lives and experiences we might never encounter otherwise. They're an accessible, universal language—a way of saying, "This is me, right now, in this moment."

In the chapters ahead, we'll explore the nitty-gritty of taking the perfect selfie: from finding your best angles to mastering editing apps. But for now, let this serve as your introduction to a world where every face has a story to tell and every photo is an opportunity to share a piece of yourself.

So grab your phone, find some good light, and remember—the perfect selfie isn't about perfection at all. It's about capturing a moment that feels true to you.

CHAPTER 2: 100 SECRETS TO SELFIE PERFECTION

Selfies aren't just pictures—they're an art form, a science, and sometimes, a full-blown adventure. In this chapter, we'll take a deep dive into 100 secrets, subtleties, and tricks that'll elevate your selfie game from "meh" to masterpiece. Let's get started with tips grouped by theme—because even a perfect selfie starts with a plan.

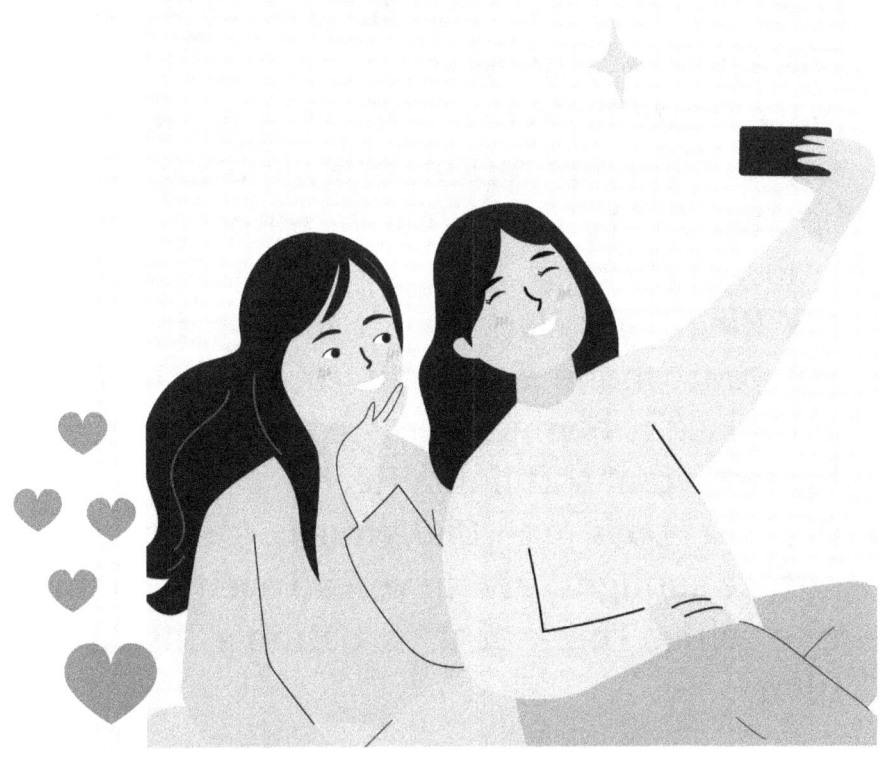

LIGHTING: THE UNSUNG HERO (TIPS 1–10)

- *Golden Hour is Your* Best Friend: Take your selfie within an hour after sunrise or an hour before sunset. The soft, golden light flatters all skin tones and adds an ethereal glow. Example: Ever noticed how your face looks like it's straight out of a music video when the sun is low? That's the golden hour magic.
- *Face the Light:* Always position yourself so the light hits your face directly, not from the side or behind. This eliminates harsh shadows and brightens your features.
- *Avoid Overhead Lighting:* Overhead lights cast unflattering shadows under your eyes and chin. Move to a softer, diffused light source, like a nearby window.
- *Make Use of Reflective Surfaces:* A white wall, a sheet of aluminum foil, or even a napkin can bounce light onto your face for a natural "glow up."
- *DIY Ring Light Hack:* Don't have a ring light? Set your phone flashlight to low brightness and place it behind a frosted bottle or tissue for an instant soft light effect.
- *Overcast Days are Underrated:* Cloudy skies diffuse sunlight, giving you an even, shadow-free selfie. Think of it as nature's Instagram filter.

- *Candlelight Glow:* For cozy, intimate selfies, use candles or a small string of fairy lights for a warm, romantic vibe.
- *Blue Hour Drama:* Right after sunset, the blue tones create an atmospheric, moody backdrop perfect for creative selfies.
- *Dim the Screen Glow:* If you're taking a late-night selfie, don't let your phone screen overexpose your face. Adjust brightness to a softer level.
- *Car Sunshades Magic:* Flip down your car's sunshade mirror and position yourself in the gentle shade—perfect lighting and a built-in mirror!

ANGLES AND COMPOSITION: YOUR SECRET WEAPON (TIPS 11–25)

- *Chin Down, Eyes Up:* Tilting your chin slightly downward while gazing into the camera gives a confident, sharp look.
- *Don't Center Yourself:* Use the rule of thirds—align your face slightly to the side of the frame for a more dynamic shot.
- *Highlight the Jawline:* Stretch your neck slightly forward to define your jaw and avoid the dreaded "selfie double chin."
- *Experiment with Angles:* Take shots from above, below, and straight-on to see which perspective best suits your face.

- *Side Profiles are Underrated:* Rotate your head 45 degrees to highlight your best side (yes, everyone has a "best" side!).
- *Arms-Length Perspective:* Holding the phone slightly farther away from your face softens proportions and prevents distortion.
- *Avoid the Up-the-Nose Shot:* We've all been there. Keep the camera at eye level or slightly above for a flattering view.
- *Diagonal Composition:* Add drama by tilting the phone slightly, so your background slants at an angle.
- *Group Selfies Rule of Thumb:* Always place the tallest person at the back and the lightest-skinned friend near the light source to balance shadows.
- *Use Your Environment:* Lean against a doorframe or sit on a windowsill to add depth and natural framing to your shot.
- *Be Aware of Backgrounds:* A clean, uncluttered background lets you shine as the star of the selfie.
- *The Power of Symmetry:* Position yourself in front of symmetrical backgrounds like doorways or arches for a professional vibe.
- *Dynamic Movement:* Flip your hair or toss a scarf mid-shot to add a sense of action.
- *Point of View Perspective:* Hold the camera lower to capture your outfit or surrounding

details for a lifestyle look.
- *The "Over-the-Shoulder" Glance:* This classic pose is perfect for showing off a killer hairstyle or dramatic lighting.

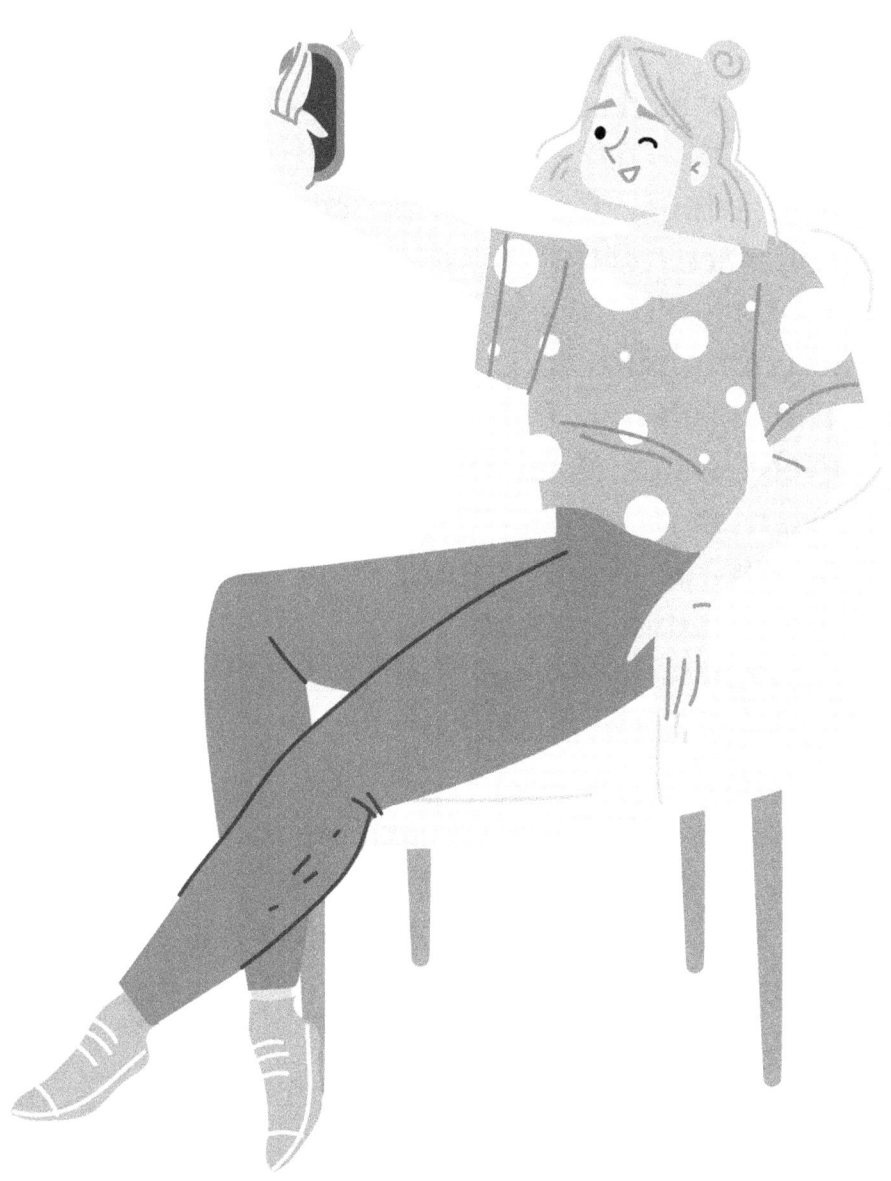

EXPRESSION: THE HEART OF A SELFIE
(TIPS 26–40)

- *Natural Smiles Win:* Fake smiles are easy to spot. Think of a funny moment to evoke a genuine grin.
- *Relax Your Face:* Avoid tensed lips or wide eyes; soft, natural expressions are more photogenic.
- *Channel Your Inner Mood:* Whether it's mysterious, cheerful, or contemplative, let your face tell the story.
- *Subtle Smirk Magic:* A slight lift in one corner of your mouth adds intrigue and confidence.
- *The Eyebrow Raise:* Slightly raising your eyebrows can make your eyes look bigger and brighter.
- *Laugh Mid-Selfie:* Capture yourself mid-laugh for a candid, joyful vibe.
- *Experiment with Lips:* Try a relaxed pout, a soft smile, or even biting your lower lip slightly for variety.
- *Close Your Eyes and Relax:* Open them slowly for a serene, dreamy expression.
- *Use Props to Break the Ice:* Hold a coffee cup, wear funky sunglasses, or twirl your hair for a natural pose.
- *Play With Hair:* Run your fingers through your hair or flip it for a carefree look.
- *Focus on Your Eyes:* Let your gaze draw viewers in. Practice looking into the camera with

purpose.
- **_Slightly Parted Lips:_** This subtle trick adds softness to your face and a touch of allure.
- **_The Classic "Lip Bite":_** Playful yet charming, it works wonders in moderation.
- **_Fake Yawns are Funny:_** Pretend to yawn—it might trigger a real laugh, and those are always photogenic.
- **_Mirror Practice:_** Spend time in front of a mirror testing expressions to find what suits you best.

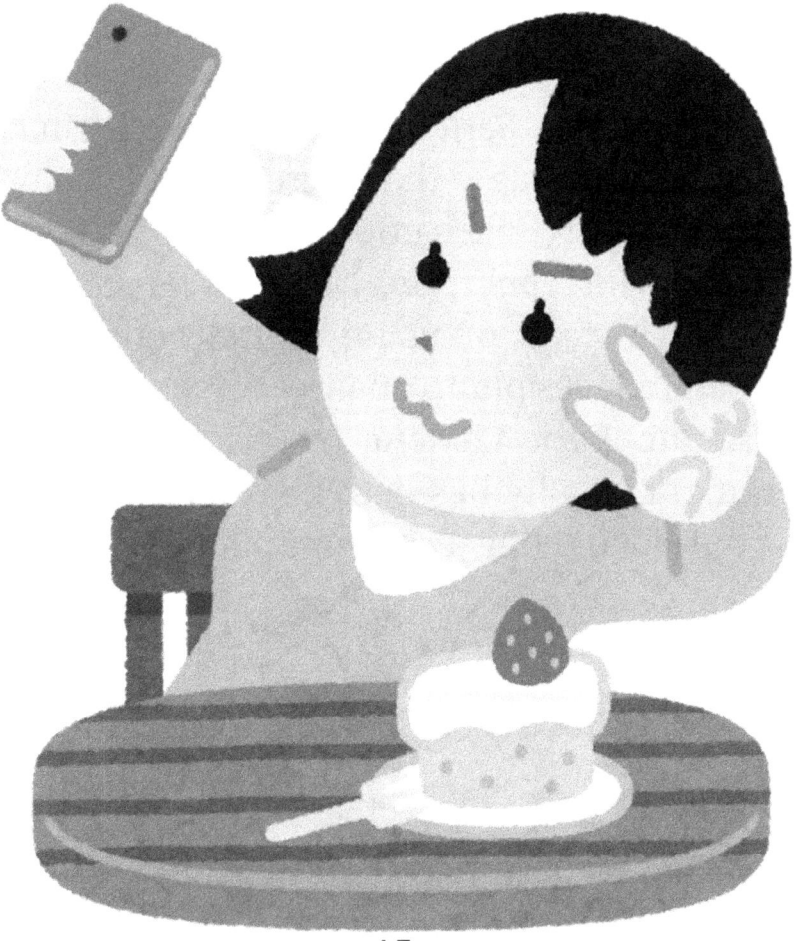

PHONE TECHNIQUES: THE ESSENTIALS
(TIPS 41–60)

- *Clean Your Camera Lens:* A quick wipe with a microfiber cloth removes smudges and ensures sharp, clear photos. Don't skip this—it's like brushing your teeth before a date!
- *Use the Timer:* Avoid shaky hands by setting a 3-second or 10-second timer. This also frees you up for better posing.
- *Burst Mode is Your BFF:* Hold down the shutter button to capture multiple shots in rapid succession—great for action poses or group selfies.
- *Portrait Mode Perfection:* Many phones have a portrait mode that creates a blurred background (bokeh effect) to make you pop.
- *Zoom with Your Feet, Not Your Fingers:* Step closer instead of using digital zoom, which often reduces photo quality.
- *Use the Back Camera for Quality:* The rear camera usually has better resolution than the front-facing one. Prop your phone up and use

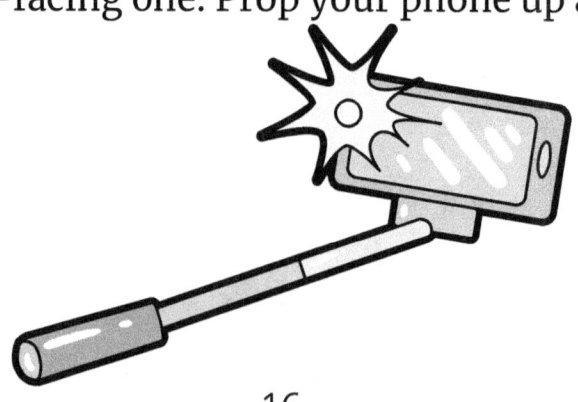

a timer for sharper selfies.
- **Lock the Focus:** Tap on your face to lock the focus and exposure so the camera doesn't adjust mid-shot.
- **Experiment with HDR:** High Dynamic Range (HDR) mode can balance tricky lighting situations, like a bright sky behind you.
- **Stabilize with Props:** Rest your phone on a sturdy surface or use a tripod for steady shots. Even a stack of books will do!
- **Voice Commands Save the Day:** Some phones let you say "cheese" or clap your hands to trigger the shutter. Perfect for hands-free selfies.
- **Use a Selfie Stick (Yes, Really):** They're not just tourist gimmicks—they give you better angles and include more background in your frame.
- **Remote Shutter Controls:** Bluetooth remotes are inexpensive and allow you to snap selfies from a distance.
- **Master Night Mode:** If your phone has night mode, experiment with it for low-light selfies. Hold very still to avoid blur.
- **Control Brightness Manually:** Swipe up or down on your screen to adjust brightness before snapping the shot.
- **Experiment with Lenses:** Clip-on lenses, like fisheye or wide-angle, can add creative flair to your selfies.

- *Get a Tripod with a Ring Light:* This combo is a game-changer for selfies, especially in dim settings.
- *Don't Forget Live Photos:* These mini-video selfies capture motion and sound, adding a layer of storytelling.
- *Flip the Phone Upside-Down:* For certain angles, flipping your phone can create a unique perspective.
- *Watch for Reflections:* If you're near a mirror or window, check for unwanted reflections of your phone in the shot.
- *Set Your Frame in Advance:* Use gridlines on your phone's screen to align yourself and compose your shot like a pro.

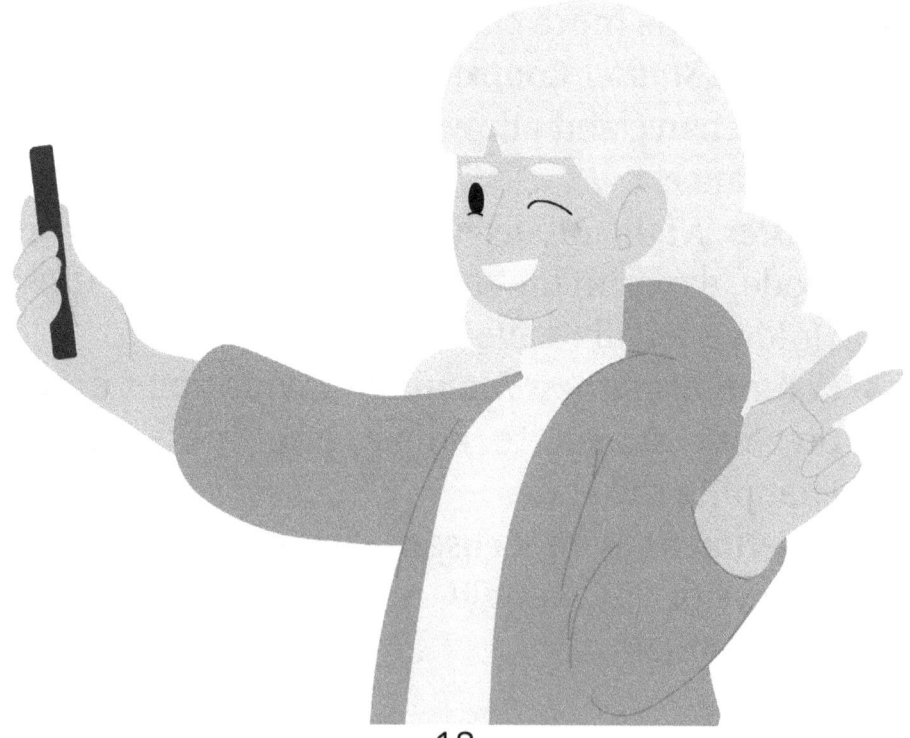

BACKGROUND MAGIC: SETTING THE SCENE (TIPS 61–75)

- *Declutter Your Space:* A messy background distracts from you. Tidy up or choose a simple, neutral backdrop.
- *Include Iconic Landmarks:* If you're traveling, angle yourself to include famous landmarks without blocking them entirely.
- *Blurred Backgrounds Add Focus:* Some apps let you blur the background after the photo, emphasizing your face.
- *Nature Always Wins:* Trees, flowers, or even a clear blue sky make for stunning, vibrant backgrounds.
- *Find Patterns:* Bricks, tiles, or artistic murals can add depth and texture to your shot.
- *Play With Perspective:* Use stairs, doorways, or hallways to create leading lines that draw attention to you.
- *Reflections are Fun:* Use mirrors, water puddles, or glass surfaces for creative compositions.
- *Add Foreground Elements:* Frame yourself with plants, curtains, or other objects in the foreground for a layered effect.
- *Experiment With Shadows:* Play with the light streaming through blinds or leaves to create artistic patterns.

- *Use Your Surroundings to Tell a Story:* A cozy coffee shop, a bustling street, or a serene beach adds context to your selfie.
- *Bright Colors Pop:* Find vibrant walls or objects that contrast with your outfit for extra visual appeal.
- *Watch for Photobombers:* A sneaky cat or a giggling friend can sometimes enhance the photo—if it's intentional.
- *Use Negative Space:* Leave plenty of empty space around you for a minimalist and modern aesthetic.
- *Create Symmetry:* Align yourself with a road, river, or symmetrical architecture for a balanced composition.
- *Background Blur Apps:* Tools like Snapseed or Photoshop Express can help tidy up distracting backgrounds.

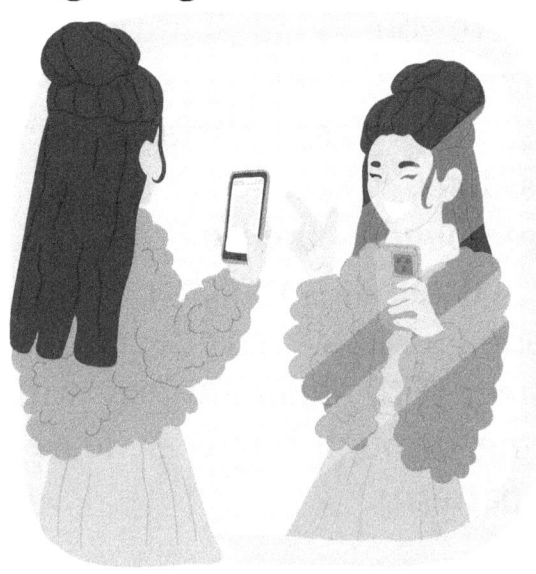

EDITING AND FILTERS: ENHANCING THE MOMENT (TIPS 76–90)

- *Edit Sparingly:* A little goes a long way—don't overdo filters or retouching, or you risk looking unnatural.
- *Brighten, Don't Overexpose:* Increase brightness slightly to enhance your selfie, but avoid blowing out highlights.
- *Use Face-Smoothing Sparingly:* Most editing apps offer this feature, but overusing it can make you look plastic.
- *Adjust Contrast for Depth:* A slight bump in contrast can make your features pop.
- *Play with Color Temperature:* Warmer tones add vibrancy, while cooler tones create a modern, sleek vibe.
- *Remove Background Clutter:* Apps like Adobe Photoshop or Canva can help erase unwanted distractions.
- *Use Blemish Tools Gently:* Editing out a pimple is fine, but keep freckles and other natural features intact.
- *Add Subtle Filters:* Apps like VSCO or Lightroom offer subtle filters that enhance without overwhelming.
- *Crop Strategically:* Tighten the frame to remove excess space and draw attention to your face.

- *Experiment with Black and White:* Sometimes, removing color highlights the emotion or texture of your photo.
- *Try Lens Flares:* Adding light flares or sparkles can give your selfie a whimsical vibe.
- *Check Before You Post:* Zoom in to ensure your edits look good at full resolution, not just on a thumbnail.
- *Keep Original Files:* Save an unedited version just in case you want to start fresh later.
- *Collages Can Tell Stories:* Combine multiple selfies or mix with scenic shots for a fun presentation.
- *Don't Skip Presets:* Apps like Lightroom offer presets to streamline editing.

CREATIVITY AND CONFIDENCE: UNLEASHING YOUR UNIQUE STYLE (TIPS 91–100)

- *Break the Rules for Fun:* Once you've mastered the basics, experiment with unconventional angles. Example: Hold your phone at waist level and look away from the camera for an artsy, candid feel. These shots often stand out because they deviate from the norm.
- *Use Props to Tell a Story:* Props can bring personality to your selfie. For instance, if you're at the beach, hold a seashell near your face, or use sunglasses as a playful accessory.

Example: Imagine holding a steaming cup of coffee on a rainy day—your breath on the glass window behind you adds mood and drama.
- Incorporate Movement: Selfies don't have to be static. Spin around, flip your hair, or sway a scarf. Example: Picture yourself at a park—throw autumn leaves in the air mid-shot. Use burst mode to capture the action and select the perfect frame later.
- Capture Silhouettes: Position yourself in front of a light source (like the setting sun) to create a dramatic silhouette selfie. Example: Raise your phone low to the ground and stand tall for a mysterious, powerful pose against the fading light.
- Include Your Hands: Posing with your hands in the frame adds interest. Example: Rest your chin on your hand or gently touch your hair. This breaks the monotony and makes your selfie look more intentional.
- Be Playful with Themes: Create selfies based on a theme. Example: If you're wearing a vintage dress, find a retro car or brick wall to match the vibe. Pose as though you're a time traveler who just stepped into the modern world.
- Mirror Selfies with a Twist: Instead of the usual straight-on mirror shot, tilt the mirror

to reflect the sky or surroundings creatively. Example: Place a handheld mirror on the ground and shoot from above, capturing the sky in the reflection with your face.
- Let Shadows Do the Work: Use shadows creatively. Example: Stand near a window with blinds to cast striped shadows across your face. Or try using a leafy plant for natural, intricate patterns.
- Add Depth with Layers: Position objects at different distances from the camera for depth. Example: Hold a translucent scarf or a frosted glass in front of the lens for a dreamy, ethereal effect.
- Own Your Confidence: The most important tip: Confidence radiates through the lens. Stand tall, smile, and believe in yourself. Example: Think of a moment that made you feel unstoppable—a recent achievement or a time when you overcame a challenge. Channel that energy, and your selfie will exude authenticity and power.

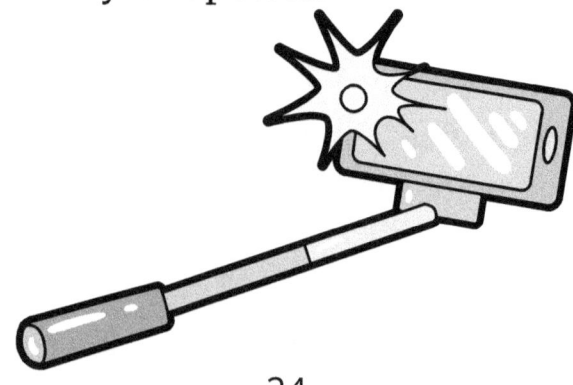

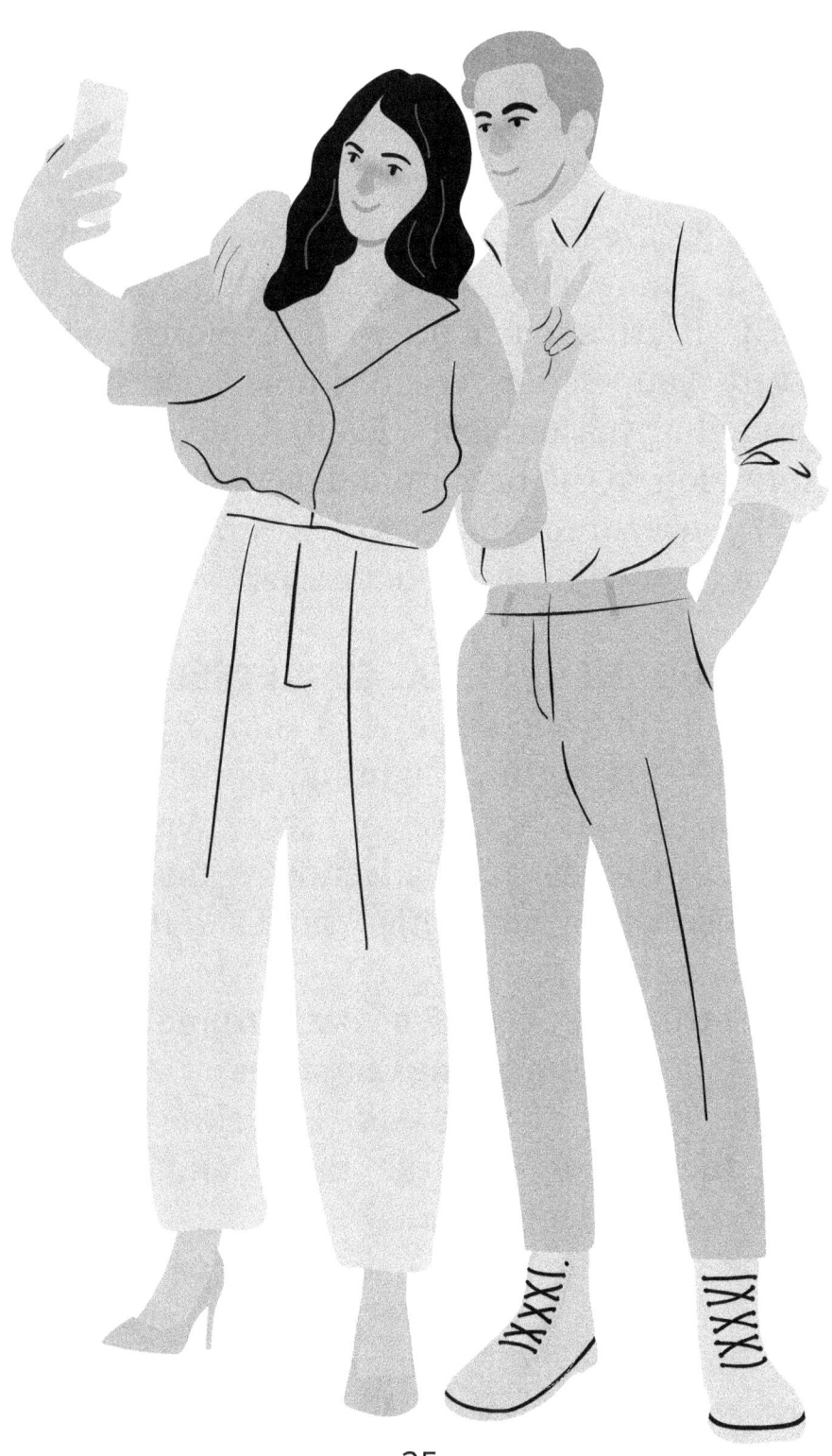

CHAPTER 3: TELLING YOUR STORY THROUGH SELFIES

Selfies are more than just pictures—they're a way to share your unique narrative with the world. In this chapter, we'll explore how to elevate your selfies from simple snapshots to storytelling masterpieces. Every detail, from your expression to the background, contributes to the story you want to tell. Let's dive into how you can craft a compelling visual narrative.

THE ART OF VISUAL STORYTELLING

Think of your selfie as a mini-novel. Each element—the setting, lighting, pose, and even the props—adds depth to your story. Whether you want to convey joy, adventure, mystery, or introspection, your selfie should reflect your emotions and intentions.

Setting the Scene: The Background as a Supporting Character

The setting of your selfie is like the backdrop of a theater—it sets the mood and provides context. Consider these ideas:

The Adventure Selfie: Use dramatic landscapes like mountains, beaches, or forests to show your love for exploration. Example: Stand on a cliff with the wind in your hair and the vast ocean behind you. Tilt your phone upward slightly to capture both yourself and the breathtaking view.

The Cozy Selfie: A soft blanket, a cup of tea, and fairy lights create a warm, inviting vibe. Example: Sit by a window on a rainy day, letting the soft natural light illuminate your face while the raindrops on the glass add texture to the scene.

The Urban Selfie: Graffiti walls, city skylines, or bustling street markets make excellent backdrops for urban storytelling. Example: Pose in front of a mural that reflects your personality, like a vibrant design for a fun vibe or a minimalist one for sophistication.

EXPRESSING EMOTION: THE HEART OF A STORY

Your expression is the core of your selfie's story. It's what draws viewers in and gives them a glimpse into your world.

Here's how to use your emotions effectively:

Joy and Excitement: Capture genuine smiles or laughter for an uplifting story. Example: Imagine you've just reunited with an old friend—let that happiness shine through as you snap the selfie.

Serenity and Peace: For a calming vibe, use soft lighting and a neutral or pastel palette. Example: Take a selfie while meditating in a quiet park, with sunlight filtering through the trees onto your face.

Mystery and Drama: Use shadows, unique angles, or a serious gaze to evoke intrigue. Example: Take a silhouette shot at sunset, with your face barely visible and the fiery sky behind you.

PROPS AND ACCESSORIES: STORYTELLING DETAILS

Props are like supporting characters in your story—they add personality and interest.

Here are a few creative ideas:

- *Books:* Holding a book suggests intellect or a love for storytelling. Example: Snap a selfie with your favorite novel while lounging on a cozy chair.
- *Food and Drinks:* Highlight cultural experiences or indulgent moments. Example: A close-up selfie with a latte art design or an exotic dish can convey your foodie adventures.
- *Nature Elements:* Flowers, leaves, or even a handful of sand can add texture and connection to the natural world. Example: Hold a single rose near your face, letting the soft petals contrast with your sharp features.

LIGHTING AND MOOD: CONTROLLING THE ATMOSPHERE

Lighting doesn't just flatter your features; it creates an emotional tone for your selfie.

Golden Hour for Warmth: Use the soft glow of the golden hour to tell a story of optimism and beauty. Example: Walk through a field, letting the sunlight highlight your hair and skin.

Candlelight for Intimacy: Candles create a romantic, cozy mood. Example: Snap a selfie at a candlelit dinner, with the flickering light dancing across your face.

Neon Lights for Edginess: Bright, colorful neon signs scream adventure and nightlife. Example: Pose near a neon sign at a bar or arcade, letting the colors reflect off your skin.

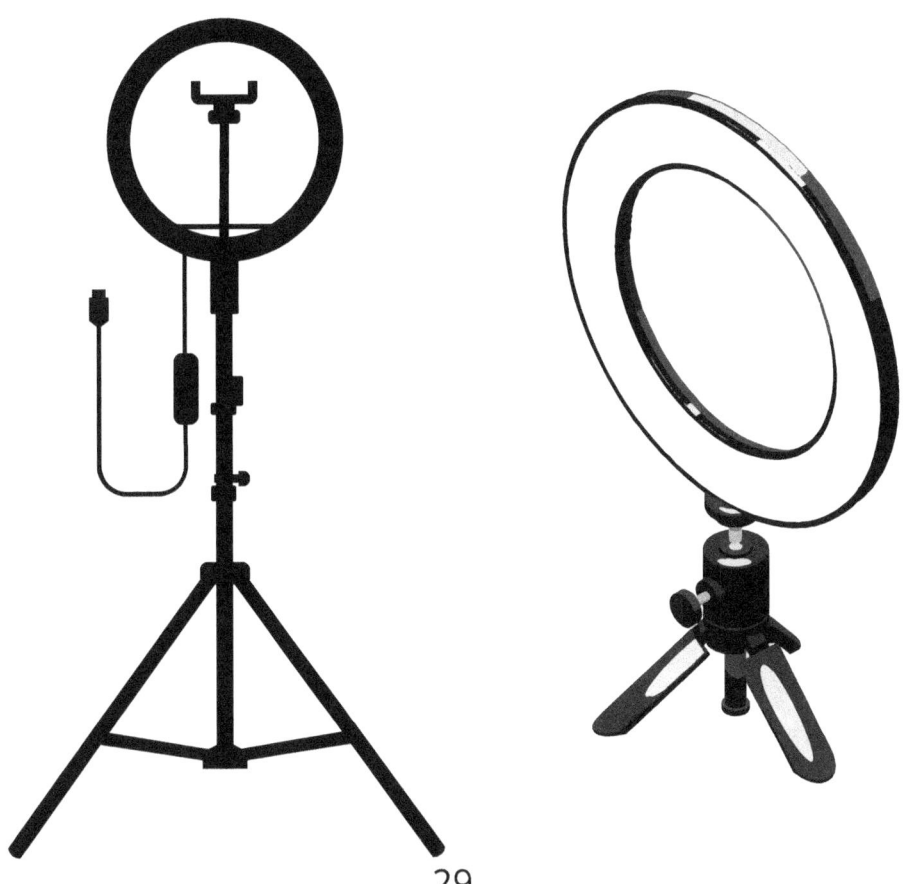

COMPOSITION AND FRAMING: DIRECTING THE VIEWER'S EYE

The way you frame your selfie guides how the story unfolds.

Leading Lines: Use elements like roads, fences, or pathways to draw the viewer's attention to you. Example: Stand at the center of a forest path, letting the trees naturally frame your face.

Foreground and Background Layers: Add depth by placing objects in the foreground, middle ground, and background. Example: Hold a clear glass near the camera to blur the edges and create a dreamy vignette.

Negative Space: Leave plenty of empty space around you for a minimalist vibe. Example: Stand alone in an open field, emphasizing solitude and reflection.

EDITING FOR STORYTELLING

Post-production can enhance your narrative without overwhelming the viewer.

Subtle Color Grading: Adjust the colors to match your story. Example: Warm tones for a nostalgic feel or cool tones for a futuristic vibe.

Selective Focus: Blur the background to keep the focus on your face. Example: If you're in a crowded city, highlight your face while keeping the hustle and bustle softly out of focus.

Creative Overlays: Use apps to add light leaks,

grain, or soft vignettes for an artistic touch. Example: Add a soft golden light overlay to a sunset selfie to enhance its dreamy quality.

CRAFTING A SERIES: A STORY IN MULTIPLE FRAMES

Sometimes, a single selfie isn't enough to tell your story. Create a series of photos to add context and depth.

Start with a Wide Shot: Show the environment you're in. Example: A full-body shot of you standing in a sunflower field.

Zoom In for Details: Highlight small elements. Example: A close-up of your hand brushing a sunflower petal.

End with a Portrait: Capture your face with the story's context in the background. Example: A selfie with the field stretching into the horizon behind you.

Selfies are an art form, a snapshot of a moment, and a window into your story. With the tools from this chapter, you can start crafting selfies that don't just look good but also speak volumes about who you are. What story will your next selfie tell?

CHAPTER 4: PROGRAMS AND APPS FOR THE PERFECT SELFIE

Technology has revolutionized the art of taking selfies. With countless apps and programs available, even a basic selfie can be transformed into a polished, eye-catching masterpiece.

In this chapter, we'll explore the best tools for selfie enhancement, how to use them effectively, and some insider secrets for maximizing their potential.

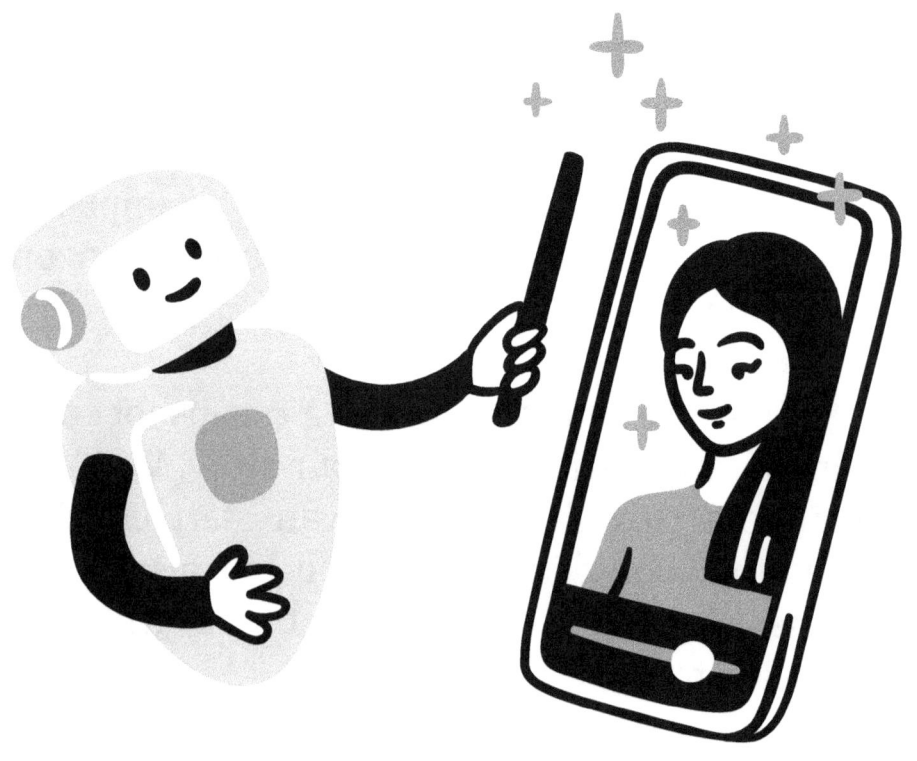

1. APPS FOR CAMERA CONTROL AND SHOOTING

Before we even get to editing, the right camera app can elevate your selfie game. These apps give you greater control over focus, lighting, and composition.

1.1. VSCO (Visual Supply Company)

Why It's Great: VSCO offers manual camera controls for adjusting focus, exposure, and white balance before you snap your selfie. It's perfect for experimenting with different moods.

Pro Tip: Use the "Grid" feature while composing your selfie to align yourself according to the rule of thirds. This ensures a more balanced shot.

1.2. Adobe Lightroom Camera

Why It's Great: This app's built-in camera mode allows RAW image capture, offering unparalleled quality for editing later.

Secret: Experiment with the "Exposure Lock" feature to maintain consistent lighting on your face, even in tricky environments.

1.3. Halide (iOS)

Why It's Great: Known for its professional-grade tools, Halide gives you complete control over shutter speed and ISO, which can make low-light selfies much clearer.

Insider Tip: Use Halide's "Depth Capture" mode for creative portrait selfies with stunning background blur.

1.4. Snapchat Camera

Why It's Great: While Snapchat is a social app, its AR (augmented reality) lenses and filters are often ahead of the curve.

Trick: Activate "lens exploration" to discover hidden or user-created lenses that add unique flair to your selfies.

2. EDITING APPS TO ENHANCE YOUR LOOK

Once your selfie is taken, the magic truly begins with editing. These apps can enhance lighting, smooth skin, and add artistic flair.

2.1. Facetune

Why It's Great: Facetune offers tools for skin smoothing, teeth whitening, and even reshaping facial features for subtle tweaks.

Secret: Don't overuse the "smooth" tool—it's tempting, but too much can make your skin look plastic. Instead, aim for small adjustments for a natural look.

2.2. Snapseed

Why It's Great: This Google-owned app features powerful yet user-friendly tools for professional-grade edits. The "Selective Adjust" feature allows you to brighten or sharpen specific areas of your selfie.

Pro Tip: Use the "Portrait" filter to add subtle enhancements to your face, like sharpening eyes or softening shadows.

2.3. AirBrush

Why It's Great: Known for its one-tap fixes, AirBrush is perfect for quick edits on the go.

Secret: Try the "Bokeh" tool to create a soft, dreamy background blur, even if your phone doesn't have portrait mode.

2.4. PicsArt

Why It's Great: This app combines robust photo editing tools with fun, creative options like stickers, doodles, and artistic effects.

Pro Tip: Use the "Dispersion" effect for a dynamic, artsy selfie. It makes parts of your face appear to dissolve into pixels—perfect for Instagram flair.

2.5. BeautyPlus

Why It's Great: This app specializes in beautification tools, offering real-time beauty filters as well as post-capture editing.

Trick: Use the "Live Beauty" mode to preview effects while snapping your selfie.

3. APPS FOR FILTERS AND AESTHETIC ENHANCEMENTS

Filters can change the entire vibe of your selfie, turning ordinary shots into works of art.

3.1. Instagram

Why It's Great: Instagram's built-in filters and editing tools are simple yet effective.

Secret: Explore AR filters in Stories. Search for

specific effects like "golden hour" or "retro film" to enhance your selfie with unique lighting or colors.

3.2. Prequel

Why It's Great: Prequel offers trendsetting filters like vintage film and 3D effects. It's perfect for creating stylish, themed selfies.

Pro Tip: Use the "Disco" filter for selfies with a shimmering, retro vibe that catches the eye.

3.3. Afterlight

Why It's Great: This app offers dozens of adjustable filters, textures, and light leaks for an artsy finish.

Trick: Layer multiple filters and textures for a one-of-a-kind look that can't be replicated elsewhere.

3.4. Lightroom Mobile

Why It's Great: Presets allow you to create consistent themes for your selfies.

Secret: Download free presets online to achieve cinematic tones, pastel vibes, or high-contrast drama.

3.5. Meitu

Why It's Great: Popular in Asia, Meitu offers whimsical filters, anime-style effects, and robust editing tools.

Pro Tip: Use the "Magic Brush" to add cute sparkles or hearts to your selfies for a playful touch.

4. AR AND AI-ENHANCED SELFIE TOOLS

Augmented reality (AR) and artificial intelligence (AI) have made selfies smarter, letting you experiment with virtual try-ons, instant beautification, and even face swaps.

4.1. *YouCam Makeup*

Why It's Great: Perfect for experimenting with makeup looks before applying them in real life.

Trick: Try bold styles you might hesitate to apply in real life—like glitter lips or dramatic eyeliner—and snap your selfie virtually.

4.2. *Lensa AI*

Why It's Great: Lensa uses AI to retouch selfies automatically while preserving a natural look.

Pro Tip: Use the "Magic Avatar" feature to generate artistic, AI-rendered versions of your selfie.

4.3. *B612*

Why It's Great: This app blends AR effects, live filters, and beauty adjustments.

Trick: Explore seasonal filters for fun, holiday-themed selfies. A snowy background? Instant holiday magic!

4.4. *FaceApp*

Why It's Great: Famous for its face-aging tool, FaceApp also has amazing lighting and smile-correction features.

Pro Tip: Use the "Makeup" mode for subtle enhancements that don't scream "edited."

4.5. Voila AI Artist

Why It's Great: Turns your selfie into a cartoon or Renaissance-style portrait using AI.

Secret: Use this for creative profile pictures or as part of a selfie series to show off your artistic side.

5. TIPS FOR MAXIMIZING THESE TOOLS

To get the most out of selfie apps, keep these pointers in mind:

- *Start Subtle:* Always begin with minimal edits and increase adjustments gradually to avoid over-editing.
- *Know Your Filters:* Familiarize yourself with filters and effects in advance so you can select the right vibe for your selfie.
- *Combine Apps:* Don't limit yourself to one app. Use one for shooting (like Halide), another for editing (Snapseed), and a third for creative enhancements (Prequel).
- *Experiment with Layers:* For artistic selfies, layer effects and filters to create a unique masterpiece.
- *Save Your Presets:* Many apps allow you to save custom editing presets, making it easy to maintain a consistent aesthetic.

By incorporating these apps into your selfie routine, you'll have the tools to create stunning images that reflect your unique style and personality. Now it's time to explore, experiment, and snap away!

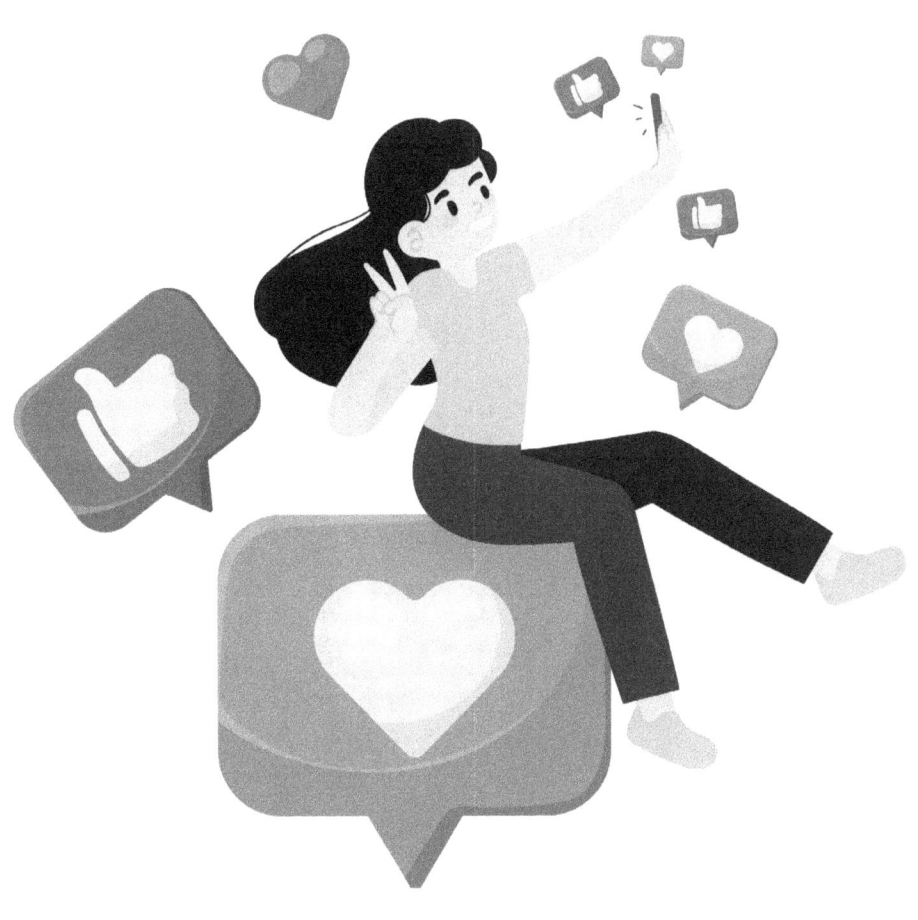

CHAPTER 5: 100 SURPRISING, SHOCKING, AND DELIGHTFUL FACTS ABOUT SELFIES

Selfies are more than just a modern pastime; they're packed with fascinating stories, surprising trends, and even a touch of danger.

In this chapter, we'll take a whirlwind tour through 100 incredible facts and real-life stories about selfies. Some are funny, some are shocking, and all are proof that selfies are as dynamic as the people taking them.

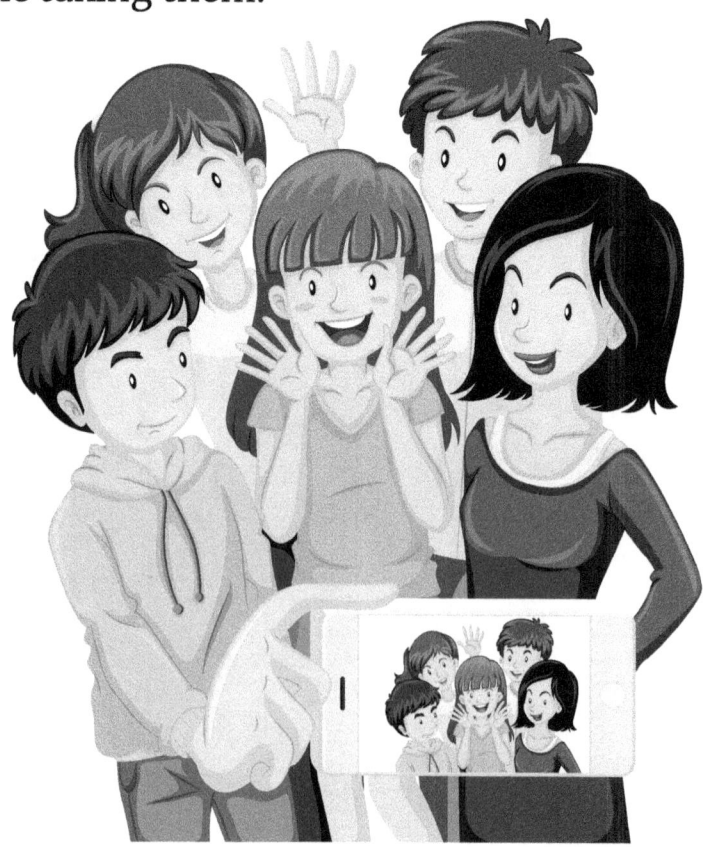

THE ORIGINS AND EVOLUTION OF SELFIES
(FACTS 1–10)

- The First "Selfie" Ever? The first known photographic selfie was taken in 1839 by Robert Cornelius, a chemist and photography enthusiast. He removed the lens cap, sprinted into the frame, and held still for several minutes. That's dedication!
- The Word's Origin: The term "selfie" was first used in 2002 on an Australian forum where a man posted a photo of himself with a busted lip, saying, "Sorry about the focus, it was a selfie." The term stuck!
- The Selfie Stick Predates Smartphones: A Japanese man named Hiroshi Ueda invented a primitive selfie stick in 1983. It was meant for a film camera, but the idea didn't catch on until smartphones came along.
- Selfie: An Official Word: In 2013, "selfie" was crowned the Oxford English Dictionary's Word of the Year. By then, the word had increased in usage by 17,000% in just 12 months.
- Mirror Selfies Before Cameras: Ancient Egyptians were arguably the first to enjoy "mirror selfies," using polished copper to check themselves out.
- The Most Expensive Selfie: In 2014, a billionaire bought a $4.3 million painting of a hand holding a phone—essentially an artistic

interpretation of a selfie.
- The First Astronaut Selfie: Buzz Aldrin took a space selfie during the Gemini 12 mission in 1966. Imagine a selfie with Earth as your backdrop!
- The Celebrity Selfie That Broke Twitter: Ellen DeGeneres' iconic Oscar selfie in 2014 featured stars like Bradley Cooper, Jennifer Lawrence, and Meryl Streep. It became the most retweeted tweet for years.
- Selfies Inspired Emoji: The popular camera emoji and selfie emoji were added to Unicode because of the selfie craze.
- The Mona Lisa of Selfies: Leonardo da Vinci's "Vitruvian Man" has been humorously dubbed the first artistic selfie due to its self-referential pose.

SELFIES AND SOCIAL MEDIA FAME (FACTS 11–20)

- The Rise of Instagram Models: Many careers have been built purely on selfies. Kylie Jenner, for example, used Instagram selfies to amass millions and launch her cosmetics empire.
- Selfie is Everywhere: On Instagram alone, the hashtag selfie has been used over 500 million times—and counting.
- Selfie Capitals of the World: Makati City in the Philippines once claimed the title of "selfie

capital," with more selfies taken there per capita than anywhere else.
- Guinness World Record for Selfies: In 2018, Dwayne "The Rock" Johnson set a record by taking 105 selfies with fans in under three minutes.
- Selfie Challenge Gone Viral: The "No Make-Up Selfie" trend raised over $8 million for cancer research in just six days. Proof that selfies can be powerful!
- Selfies Boost Confidence: Studies suggest that taking selfies can enhance self-esteem—when done in moderation.
- Selfie Addiction is Real: "Selfitis" is the term psychologists use for obsessive selfie-taking. While not officially a mental health disorder, it's been studied extensively.
- Dangerous Lengths for a Like: Influencers have climbed skyscrapers, hung off cliffs, and even swum with sharks to take the "ultimate" selfie.
- Snapchat Selfie Lenses Craze: The introduction of dog ears and rainbow vomit lenses made Snapchat the king of quirky selfie filters.
- Celebrities Love Filters Too: Even A-listers like Kim Kardashian and Selena Gomez admit to using filters to enhance their selfies.

SELFIES AND DANGER: THE RISKY SIDE (FACTS 21–30)

- The Risky Business of Selfies: Between 2011 and 2017, over 250 people worldwide died while attempting extreme selfies.
- Death by Cliffside Selfies: In 2018, a couple fell to their deaths in Yosemite National Park while trying to capture a selfie on a cliff.
- The "Tiger Selfie" Ban: Zoos around the world banned tourists from taking "tiger selfies" after numerous accidents involving the big cats.
- Selfie and Driving? A Deadly Combo: Studies have shown that taking selfies while driving is just as dangerous as texting.
- Mount Everest Selfies: While breathtaking, selfies on Everest can be perilous. Frostbite and oxygen deprivation are real risks.
- Plane Cockpit Selfies: Multiple pilots have been fined or fired for taking selfies mid-flight. Safety first!
- Train Track Selfies: Tragically, many people have been hit by trains while posing on tracks for dramatic shots.
- Selfie with a Bull: In Spain, thrill-seekers have attempted selfies during bull runs—unsurprisingly leading to injuries.
- Lightning Strike Selfies: In 2015, a British man survived a lightning strike he was attempting

to photograph.
- "Death by Selfie" Tours: Some locations, like the Grand Canyon, are now labeled "selfie danger zones" due to frequent accidents.

SELFIES IN SCIENCE AND TECHNOLOGY (FACTS 31–40)

- NASA's Rover Selfies: The Mars rovers regularly send back selfies, showing their dusty, robotic faces against alien landscapes.
- Medical Selfies Save Lives: Dermatologists now use patient-submitted selfies to monitor moles and skin conditions remotely.
- AI Learns from Selfies: Companies like Google and Apple have trained facial recognition software on millions of selfies.
- Facial Symmetry Studies: Scientists analyze selfies to study how facial symmetry impacts perceptions of beauty.
- Selfie-Powered Makeup Apps: Apps like YouCam let users "try on" makeup virtually using augmented reality and selfies.
- Selfie-Diagnosed Illness: In 2020, researchers developed an app to detect anemia through selfie analysis.
- Fitness Progress Selfies: Fitness trainers encourage selfie logs to track transformation journeys.

- The Selfie Stick: A Technological Triumph: By 2015, over 100 million selfie sticks had been sold worldwide.
- Selfie Satellites: Some companies offer to launch your selfie into space as part of a larger satellite image.
- Underwater Selfies: Waterproof phone cases allow people to capture underwater worlds, from coral reefs to shipwrecks.

FUNNY AND BIZARRE SELFIE STORIES (FACTS 41–50)

- Selfie with a President: In 2014, a Boston Red Sox player snapped a selfie with Barack Obama, making national headlines.
- Penguin Photobomb: A tourist in Antarctica took a selfie with a penguin waddling perfectly into frame.
- Giraffe Selfie Fame: A zookeeper's selfie with a photobombing giraffe went viral for the animal's hilarious expression.
- Selfie Statue: The town of Sugar Land, Texas, has a bronze statue of two women taking a selfie.
- The "Duck Face" Craze: A trend that dominated early selfies, the duck face became both iconic and ridiculed.
- Selfie with a Thief: A tourist in Bali took a selfie with the thief who later stole their

wallet!
- Monkey Selfie Legal Battle: A monkey famously snapped a selfie using a photographer's camera, sparking debates about copyright.
- Selfie with a Ghost: A woman in the UK claims her selfie captured a ghostly figure standing behind her.
- The Selfie Queen: Kim Kardashian released a book of selfies titled Selfish, proving selfies can be profitable.
- Selfie with a Shark: A diver once captured an unbelievable selfie with a great white shark looming in the background.

SELFIES IN POP CULTURE AND ENTERTAINMENT (FACTS 51–65)

- A Selfie in Space Movies: In Gravity, Sandra Bullock's character takes a selfie in zero gravity, inspiring space enthusiasts to recreate it on Earth.
- The Selfie that Launched a Career: Justin Bieber's rise to fame was partially fueled by early selfies and personal YouTube videos shared with fans.
- Selfies in Music Videos: The Chainsmokers' hit song "#SELFIE" humorously highlighted the obsession with taking the perfect selfie in club culture.

- Animated Selfies: Disney movies like Zootopia and Ralph Breaks the Internet show characters taking selfies, reflecting real-world trends.
- Superhero Selfies: Marvel's Spider-Man games let players take selfies in costume, adding a fun layer to gameplay.
- Celebrity Selfie Obsessed: Jennifer Lopez's selfie game is so strong, fans nicknamed her "The Queen of Glow" for her perfect lighting choices.
- Selfie Cameos in TV Shows: In Black Mirror's "Nosedive," selfies symbolize the characters' obsession with social media approval.
- The Royal Selfie Ban: The British Royal Family avoids taking selfies with fans, citing protocol—but a sneaky fan once captured a selfie with Prince Harry.
- Animated Selfie Filters: Apps like Snapchat and Instagram have made animated filters—think bunny ears and sparkly eyes—a selfie staple.
- The Horror Movie Selfie: Movies like Unfriended and Friend Request use creepy selfies as part of their spooky storytelling.
- Selfie with a Zombie: At themed events like zombie runs or haunted houses, people now queue to take selfies with actors in full undead makeup.

- The Oscar Selfie That Almost Didn't Happen: Ellen DeGeneres revealed that Bradley Cooper had to stretch his arm uncomfortably to capture the star-packed selfie at the Oscars in 2014.
- Selfies in Memes: Remember "Disaster Girl"? Her photo became an iconic meme, showing how selfies can take on a life of their own.
- TikTok Selfie Trends: Challenges like the "Wipe It Down" trend blend selfies with video effects for creative reveals.
- Animated Selfie Avatars: Apps like Bitmoji let users create cartoon versions of their selfies for use in chats and social media.

SELFIES BREAKING RECORDS (FACTS 66–75)
- The Most Retweeted Selfie: Ellen's Oscar selfie held the title for years until BTS fans launched their group selfies to the top.
- The Highest Selfie: A climber snapped a selfie on the summit of Mount Everest, 29,032 feet above sea level.
- The Deepest Selfie: Divers captured a selfie at the bottom of the Mariana Trench—over 36,000 feet underwater.
- The Longest Selfie Stick: The record for the longest selfie stick is 18 meters (about 59 feet) and was used in China to capture a massive group selfie.

- Largest Group Selfie: The largest recorded group selfie involved over 2,500 people at a college event in India.
- Fastest Selfie Marathon: A man in Dubai took over 1,800 selfies in an hour to break the Guinness World Record.
- The Selfie on Mars: NASA's Perseverance rover takes regular selfies to document its journey on the red planet, making it a cosmic selfie legend.
- The First Selfie in Art History: Frida Kahlo's self-portraits are often considered the original selfies for their raw emotion and personal storytelling.
- Oldest Verified Selfie: A photo of a Russian Duchess from 1914, taken in a mirror, is often cited as one of the oldest mirror selfies in existence.
- Selfie on the Edge of Space: A team of students sent a GoPro into near space attached to a weather balloon, snapping selfies as it ascended.

BIZARRE AND UNEXPECTED SELFIE STORIES (FACTS 76–80)

- Selfie at a Funeral: The "funeral selfie" trend briefly went viral, sparking debates over whether it's ever appropriate to take selfies at solemn events.

- Pet Selfies are a Thing: Apps like PetCam allow pets to "take selfies" by attracting their attention to the screen with sounds or animations.
- The Prank Selfie: A man once tricked his friend into believing he met Beyoncé by photoshopping a selfie with her. It went viral before the truth came out.
- A Selfie with Nature's Fury: A storm chaser captured a selfie with a tornado in the background. Thankfully, he survived to tell the tale!
- The Museum Disaster: A visitor once tried to take a selfie with a statue in a museum, knocking it over and causing thousands of dollars in damage.

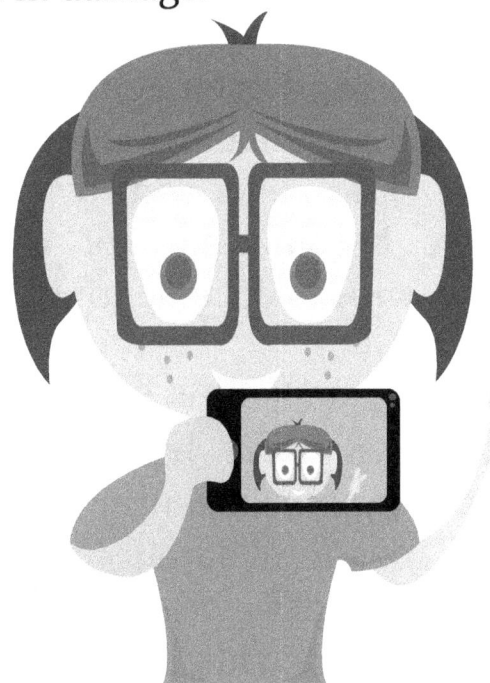

MORE INTERESTING FACTS (FACTS 81–100)

- The Selfie that Solved a Crime: In 2015, a Canadian woman was charged with murder after police discovered her selfie on social media. The photo revealed her wearing the same belt that was later used as evidence in the crime. This chilling example shows how selfies can sometimes reveal more than we intend.
- A Selfie Worth Millions : Kim Kardashian's 2015 book Selfish, a collection of her most iconic selfies, became a bestseller. Love her or not, this book proved that selfies can be a profitable art form—if you're a global icon with a loyal fan base.
- The Disaster Selfie Craze: People have a bizarre habit of snapping selfies in the face of disaster. In 2014, a man took a selfie as a raging wildfire engulfed the landscape behind him. While risky and controversial, these selfies have become part of the modern obsession with documenting dramatic moments.
- The Hollywood Celebrity Selfie Ban: Some Hollywood stars have banned fan selfies. Emma Watson, for instance, avoids taking selfies with fans to maintain her privacy and avoid exposing her location online. This highlights the dark side of the selfie culture

for public figures.
- The Bear Selfie Phenomenon: In 2014, a strange trend emerged where people took selfies dangerously close to bears in the wild. Parks in the U.S. were forced to issue warnings like, "Don't take selfies with bears," after several near-death encounters.
- Selfie Snitches: Social media selfies have landed many people in hot water. In one case, a burglar was caught because he posted a selfie from the house he was robbing, complete with stolen goods visible in the background.
- The Selfie Drone Trend: Selfie-taking drones, also known as "dronies," have grown in popularity. These gadgets allow users to capture sweeping, cinematic selfies from incredible angles. Example: A beachgoer in Bali captured a stunning dronie of themselves surrounded by turquoise waves and white sand.
- Selfies at Sacred Sites: Tourists snapping selfies at sacred or historical sites have sparked outrage. Example: In 2015, a woman faced backlash for taking a playful selfie at Auschwitz concentration camp, a location of profound historical tragedy. This highlights the ethical questions surrounding where and when selfies are appropriate.

- Selfie-Taking Pets: A gorilla named Ndakasi, who lived in a sanctuary in the Congo, went viral after photobombing a ranger's selfie. Standing upright with a casual expression, she became an internet sensation, showing that animals can sometimes steal the selfie spotlight.
- Selfies to Fight Poaching: On a positive note, rangers in Africa began taking selfies with rescued animals to raise awareness and funds for conservation. One viral campaign featured a ranger posing with giraffes, lions, and even an orphaned elephant.
- The World's First Political Selfie: In 2013, Denmark's Prime Minister Helle Thorning-Schmidt took a selfie with Barack Obama and David Cameron during Nelson Mandela's memorial service. While intended as lighthearted, the photo sparked debates about decorum at solemn events.
- The Mars Selfie: NASA's Curiosity rover on Mars captured its first selfie in 2012. The panoramic selfie stitched together several images to show the rover against the Martian landscape. This sparked a trend of space-related selfies, from astronauts to satellites.
- Selfie Controversies in Art Museums: Some museums have banned selfies altogether, citing damage caused by selfie-takers.

- Selfie Addictions Make Headlines: In 2014, a British teenager made headlines for taking over 200 selfies a day, struggling with "selfitis." This obsession highlights how selfie culture can sometimes lead to unhealthy behaviors.
- The Shark Tank Selfie: One daring tourist snapped a selfie while diving in a shark tank. Though encased in a safety cage, the proximity of the shark behind them created an adrenaline-fueled viral moment.
- The Eiffel Tower Ban: Visitors to the Eiffel Tower in Paris were asked to refrain from taking selfies while on the glass floor observation deck to prevent crowding and accidents. The rule didn't stop tourists from sneaking a shot or two, proving that selfies are nearly unstoppable.
- Selfies at the South Pole: Adventurers reaching the South Pole often celebrate the achievement with a selfie. Example: Explorer Ben Saunders snapped a frosty selfie after completing a record-breaking solo trek across Antarctica in 2014.
- Selfie Filters and Identity: Psychologists have raised concerns over selfie filters altering self-perception, especially in teens. Studies show that constant use of beauty-enhancing filters can distort how people see themselves

in real life.
- The Wedding Proposal Selfie: Creative couples have turned selfies into proposal moments. Example: A man in Italy proposed by taking a selfie in front of the Leaning Tower of Pisa, capturing his partner's shocked reaction as he held up the ring mid-photo.
- The Mona Lisa Selfie Trend: Tourists at the Louvre have turned taking selfies with the Mona Lisa into a rite of passage. The challenge? Getting a shot without dozens of heads in the background, as the crowd is always massive.

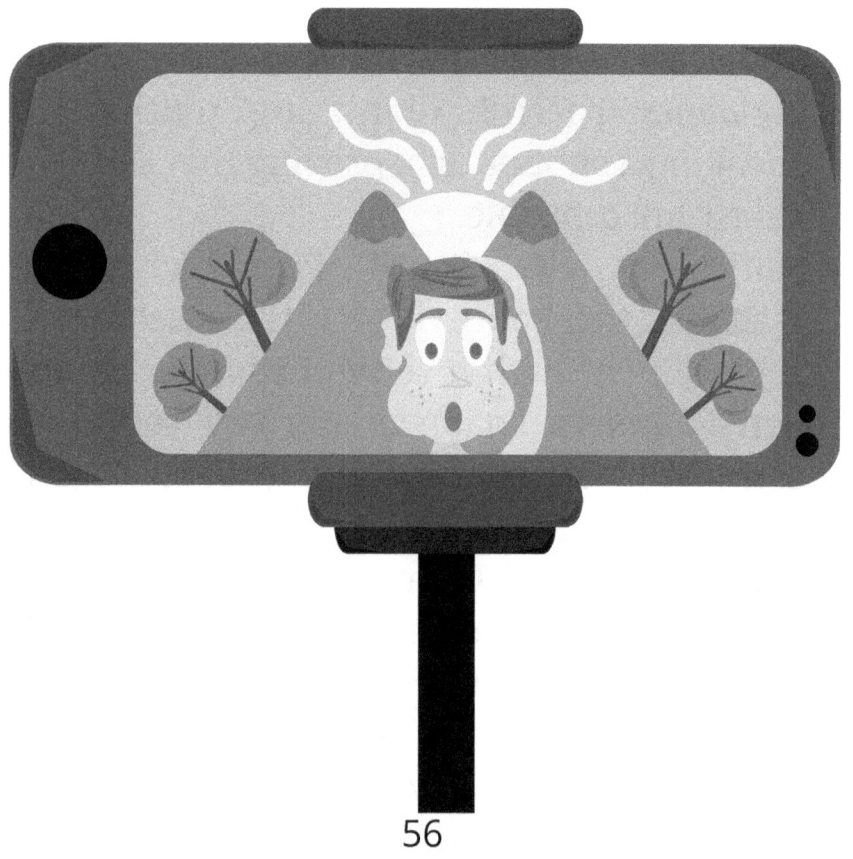

FINAL PART: THE ART OF BEING SEEN

As we close this journey into the world of selfies, it's clear that this simple act of capturing ourselves goes far beyond the surface. A selfie is more than just a picture; it's a declaration of presence, a snapshot of a moment, and sometimes, a bridge connecting us to others. From mastering lighting and angles to discovering the rich history and fascinating stories behind selfies, you now hold the tools to elevate your skills—and your confidence.

Selfies as Self-Expression

At its core, a selfie is an act of self-expression. It's a way to say, "This is who I am, in this moment." Whether you're sharing joy, creativity, vulnerability, or adventure, your selfies are a reflection of your unique identity.

Think about it: every time you take a selfie, you're freezing a fleeting second in time—a memory that might otherwise blur into the day-to-day rush. It's a form of storytelling that only you can tell.

What We've Learned

Over the chapters, we've explored everything from the technical skills of capturing the perfect selfie to the cultural impact of this phenomenon. Let's recap some key takeaways:

The Perfect Shot: Mastering lighting, angles, and composition is the foundation of any great selfie. Remember the golden hour, the power of eye-level framing, and how small tweaks can make a world of difference.

Creative Expression: Selfies are your canvas. Whether using filters, props, or dramatic backgrounds, let your creativity shine. Experiment, have fun, and don't be afraid to break the rules.

The Bigger Picture: Selfies connect us. From Ellen's viral Oscar moment to conservationists raising awareness, selfies are more than just photos—they're tools for communication and connection.

The Stories Behind the Lens: Whether it's a selfie from space or one that made history, these stories remind us of the power selfies hold to inspire, surprise, and sometimes shock us.

The Role of Technology: Modern apps and tools make it easier than ever to enhance and elevate your selfies, but the most important ingredient is always your authenticity.

Embracing Imperfection

Not every selfie will be perfect—and that's okay. In fact, some of the most memorable selfies are those that embrace imperfections, capturing moments of genuine laughter, messy hair, or unexpected photobombs. These are the selfies that tell the real story of your life.

As you continue your selfie journey, remember

that it's not about striving for perfection but celebrating who you are.

Your Next Step

Now it's your turn to create, explore, and share. Try out the tips and techniques in this book, experiment with new ideas, and keep pushing the boundaries of your creativity. Your selfies are part of your personal narrative—unique, dynamic, and always evolving.

So grab your phone, strike a pose, and step into your light. The world is waiting to see your masterpiece.

"The best selfie isn't the one that's perfect—it's the one that feels true to you."

Thank you for joining us on this journey. Here's to capturing the best version of yourself, one selfie at a time.

www.ingramcontent.com/pod-product-compliance
Lightning Source LLC
Chambersburg PA
CBHW070415230526
45471CB00006B/2814